STECK-VAUGHN

CRITICAL THINKING

Reading, Thinking, and Reasoning Skills

Authors

Don Barnes
Professor of Education
Ball State University; Muncie, Indiana

Arlene Burgdorf
Former Resource Consultant
Hammond Indiana Public Schools

L. Stanley Wenck
Professor of Educational Psychology
Ball State University; Muncie, Indiana

Consultant

Gloria Sesso
Supervisor of Social Studies
Half Hollow Hills School District; Dix Hills, New York

	LEVEL				
A	B	C	D	E	F

STECK-VAUGHN
ELEMENTARY · SECONDARY · ADULT · LIBRARY

A Harcourt Company

www.steck-vaughn.com

ACKNOWLEDGMENTS

Executive Editor: Elizabeth Strauss

Project Editor: Anita Arndt

Consulting Editor: Melinda Veatch

Design, Production, and Editorial Services: The Quarasan Group, Inc.

Contributing Writers: Tara McCarthy
Linda Ward Beech

Cover Design: Linda Adkins Graphic Design

Text:

Every effort has been made to trace the ownership of all copyrighted material and to secure the necessary permission to reprint these selections. In the event of any question arising as to the use of any material, the editor and publisher, while expressing regret for any inadvertent error, will be happy to make the necessary correction in future printings.

"One, one Cinnamon bun" reprinted with permission of Philomel Books and Curtis Brown, Ltd. from CATCH ME & KISS ME & SAY IT AGAIN, text © 1978 by Clyde Watson.

"Pie Problem" (p. 164) from A LIGHT IN THE ATTIC by Shel Silverstein. Copyright © 1981 by Evil Eye Music, Inc. Reprinted with permission of HarperCollins and Edite Kroll Literary Agency.

"thrickle" reprinted with permission of Moffitt-Lee Productions and Macmillan Publishing Company from SNIGLETS by Rich Hall and Friends. Copyright © 1984 by Not the Network Company, Inc.

Photography:
p. 5   — Nita Winter
p. 28   — D. Gordon/The Image Bank West
p. 29   — Rick Reinhard
p. 53   — Nita Winter
p. 75   — H. Armstrong Roberts

Illustration:
pp. 6, 7, 23, 48, — Linda Hawkins
pp. 8, 12, 13, 15, 16, 20, 21, 26, 33, 41, 42, 44, 50, 57, 62, 63, 66, 68, 70, 88, 90, 92 — Scott Bieser
pp. 9, 19, 22, 25, 32, 39, 43, 46, 49, 56, 59, 76, 81, 86, 91, 94 — Lynn McClain
pp. 10, 82, 93 — Peg Dougherty
pp. 11, 18, 24, 27, 28, 35, 45, 51, 52, 58, 61, 65, 71, 73, 74, 95, 96, — Kenneth Smith
pp. 14, 17, 37, 47, 69, 77 — Bill Ogden
pp. 36, 85 — Nancy Walter
pp. 38, 60, 78, — Elizabeth Allen

ISBN 0–8114–6601–9

TABLE OF CONTENTS

TABLE OF CONTENTS

Knowing

Knowing means getting the facts together. Let's try it out. Look at the girl in the picture. Do you think she's happy? Why or why not? Is she smiling? How can you tell?

Find the pictures of two things that belong in each box. Write their letters on the lines in the box.

1.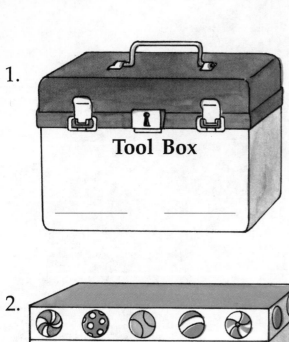
Tool Box

a.  b.

2.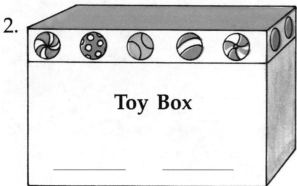
Toy Box

c. 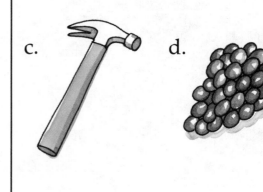 d.

3.
Lunch Box

e.  f.

Name

Look at each numbered picture on the left. Find two pictures on the right that show something like it. Write their names on the lines.

1.  _____
   _____

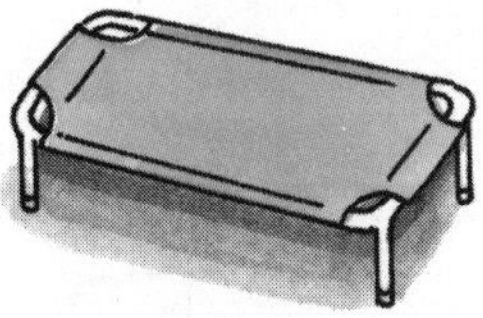

bus

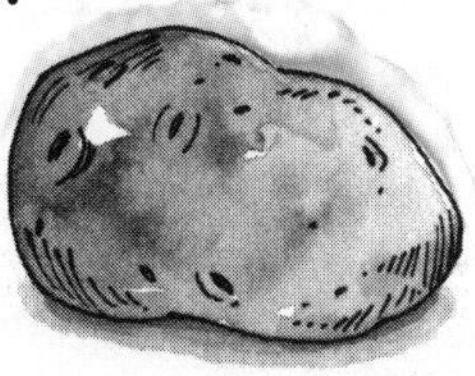

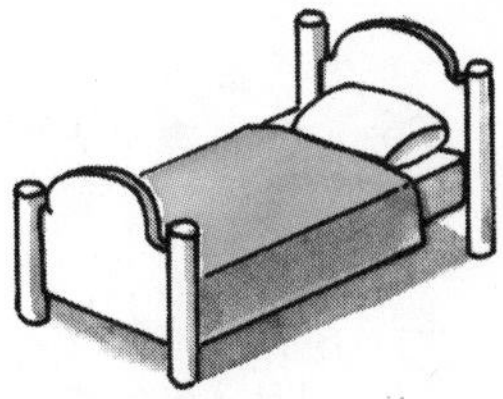

bed

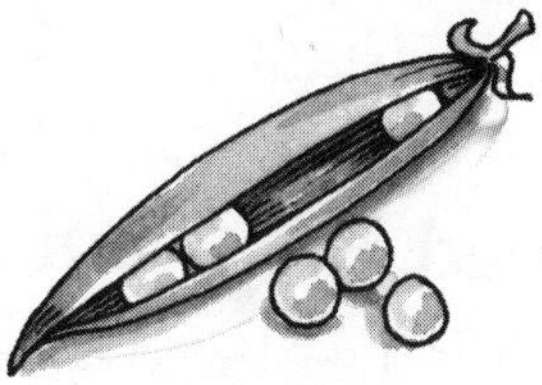

2. _____
   _____

peas

sandal

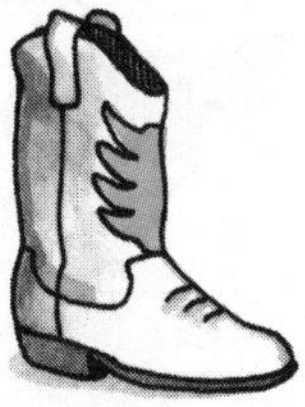

3. _____
   _____

boot

crib

4. _____
   _____

bicycle

cat

5. _____
   _____

hamster

corn

Name _____

Where can you find the things written on the fish? Write each word under the hook that tells where each thing should go.

Bedroom

Bathroom

Kitchen

Name _____

Critical Thinking, Level B © 1993 Steck-Vaughn

Read each sentence. Find the word in the **Word Box** that fits in the blank. Write the letter of that word.

Word Box

A. bug	B. dish	C. car	D. numbers
E. clothing	F. toy	G. meat	H. fruit

1. A  is one of a group of ____.

2. A ⬛ is a kind of ____.

3. A ⬛ is a kind of ____.

4. A ⬛ is a kind of ____.

5. A ⬛ is a kind of ____.

6. A ⬛ is a kind of ____.

7. A ⬛ is a kind of ____.

8. A ⬛ is a kind of ____.

Name _____

Find the two words that go with each picture. Write the letters of the two words on the lines.

1. A. bird
    B. chair
    C. top
    D. robin
    E. poodle
    F. furniture
    G. toy
    H. dog
    I. clothes
    J. jacket

2. A. tulip
    B. cat
    C. apple
    D. jewelry
    E. flower
    F. house
    G. fruit
    H. building
    I. animal
    J. ring

Name

10

Circle the sentences that tell about something make-believe. Put an **X** on the picture that shows something real.

1. Horses go to bed when they are sick.

2. Some trees grow upside down.

3. Some pigs have five legs and a cap.

4. A man and a boy can row a boat.

5. A squirrel can row a boat.

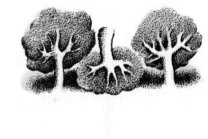

Name

11

Put an **R** before the things that are real. Put an **M** before the things that are make-believe.

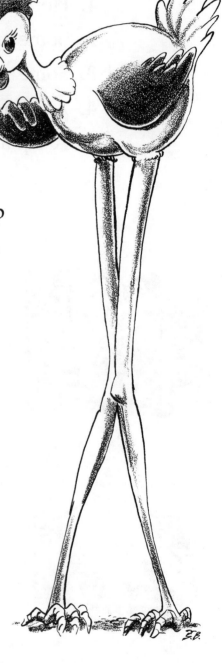

_____ 1. a fairy godmother

_____ 2. a plant with thorns

_____ 3. a brown lizard

_____ 4. a purple leopard

_____ 5. a hen with legs four feet long

_____ 6. a pencil that writes with no help

_____ 7. a brown-and-white spotted cow

_____ 8. a dancing pig

_____ 9. a magic wand

_____ 10. a twenty-foot tall giant

_____ 11. orange raindrops

_____ 12. a cow that flies without a plane

_____ 13. a white rose

_____ 14. a three-foot-high apple

_____ 15. a chair that stays outside

Name _____

Critical Thinking, Level B © 1993 Steck-Vaughn

Write **M** if the sentence tells something make-believe. Write **R** if it tells something real. Then match each sentence on the left to one on the right that tells about the same thing.

__M__   1. A giant scared Sam.

_____   2. Mice paint houses.

_____   3. The pumpkin sang.

_____   4. I play with an elf.

_____   5. The frog jumped.

_____   6. Juan watched a game.

_____   7. A dog barks at me.

_____   8. Stars shine at night.

_____   9. He bought a pan.

_____ 10. Our cat washes cars.

A. A frog became a prince.

B. We like pumpkin pie.

C. Stars fell on his head.

D. Giants are in the story.

E. The dog danced a polka.

F. Juan saw three goblins.

G. A cat washes its face.

H. Mice run in old houses.

I. The pan laughed loudly.

J. An elf was in my dream.

Name

Ann  These children like to tell stories. Ann tells stories about things that really can happen. Mike likes to tell make-believe stories. Mike

Copy each sentence below under the correct heading.

I saw a purple dog.
My sister tells funny stories.
My lizard has four legs.

My house is made of peanut butter.
I often drink milk while eating.
A sock gets hungry at lunchtime.

Real　　　　　　　　　　**Make-believe**

_____　　_____

_____　　_____

_____　　_____

_____　　_____

_____　　_____

Name

Critical Thinking, Level B © 1993 Steck-Vaughn

Write **F** before each sentence that tells a fact. Write **O** before each sentence that tells an opinion.

_____   1. Rabbits run faster than turtles.

_____   2. Pencils are used for writing.

_____   3. This peach is the best peach in the world.

_____   4. Climbing trees is not a good thing to do.

_____   5. Dinosaurs lived long ago.

_____   6. My kitten is prettier than your kitten.

_____   7. Babies are smaller than mothers.

_____   8. That juice is too sweet.

_____   9. Hammers and saws are tools.

_____   10. Some shoes are made of leather.

_____   11. Bananas taste better than apples.

_____   12. Cats are not as friendly as dogs.

_____   13. There are many different kinds of cars.

_____   14. That barn is too big and ugly.

_____   15. Rob's picture is better than mine.

Name

A. Draw a line from each fact sentence to an opinion sentence on the same subject.

Facts

1. Most people have hair.
2. Thanksgiving is a holiday.
3. Horses have four legs.
4. People need food.
5. Baseball is a game.
6. Bicycles have wheels.
7. A blue jay is a bird.
8. My mom drives to work.

Opinions

A. Riding a horse is dangerous.
B. Lunch is the best meal of the day.
C. Bluejays are too noisy.
D. Red hair is the most beautiful.
E. Everyone should have a bicycle.
F. It's easy to drive a car.
G. Thanksgiving is the best day of all.
H. The rules of baseball are easy.

B. Look at the hat. Then write two sentences of your own.

1. A **fact** about the hat:

_____

2. My **opinion** about the hat:

_____

Name

Critical Thinking, Level B © 1993 Steck-Vaughn

Read the story. Underline the three sentences that tell opinions.

Our class gave a Book Fair. We set up booths in the hallway. Each booth was for a different kind of book. I think the mystery story booth was the most interesting.

We made posters and signs for our Book Fair. I think my poster was the best one. Carol and Mike painted a sign that was bigger than any of the others.

Every class in the school visited the fair. It was the best Book Fair in the whole wide world!

Name

17

Finish the two sentences beside each picture. Make one sentence tell a fact. Make the other sentence tell your opinion.

Fact: The riders _____

Opinion: Biking is _____

Fact: The girls _____

Opinion: Jumping is _____

Fact: The boys _____

Opinion: I think _____

Fact: The children _____

Opinion: Camping is _____

Name

Critical Thinking, Level B © 1993 Steck-Vaughn

A. On each line, write the number of the correct word from the **Word Box**.

_____ grows on a tree

_____ lives but is not a plant

_____ holds many things inside

_____ holds water and other drinks

_____ something to play with

Word Box

1. animal
2. box
3. toy
4. leaf
5. cup

B. Which word in the Word Box goes with each picture? Write the number of the word on the line.

_____

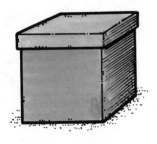

_____   _____   _____

Name _____

A. On each line, write the number of the correct word from the **Word Box**.

Word Box

_____ These are growing things with leaves.

_____ These are part of the alphabet.

_____ You stay in them.

_____ It helps you to grow.

1. food
2. letters
3. plants
4. buildings

B. On each line, write the number of a word from the Word Box. You will use each number more than once.

_____

_____

_____

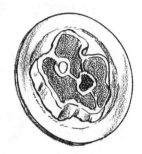
_____

_____

_____

_____

_____

Name _____

Critical Thinking, Level B © 1993 Steck-Vaughn

Read each definition and the examples. Circle the word that names the example shown in the picture.

1. a covering for the head

   scarf
   hat
   helmet

2. an animal with wings

   butterfly
   bird
   bat

3. a tool for writing

   crayon
   pencil
   pen

4. a round toy

   yoyo
   marble
   ball

5. a yellow fruit

   banana
   lemon
   pear

6. a sea animal

   seal
   fish
   dolphin

Name _____

Read the word under each picture. Write the word under the correct definition.

1. a tool for writing

_____

_____

_____

swan   hammer

pencil   duck

2. a tool used by builders

_____

_____

_____

nail   saw

3. a bird that can swim

_____

_____

_____

pen   crayon

pelican

Name _____

Critical Thinking, Level B © 1993 Steck-Vaughn

Look at the two clowns. Write words from the box to tell about each clown.

big hat

happy face

big pants

short

tall

no hair

sad face

tiny hat

small coat

curly hair

Bud the Clown

1. _____

2. _____

3. _____

4. _____

5. _____

Babs the Clown

1. _____

2. _____

3. _____

4. _____

5. _____

Name _____

23

Read each story. Then write the most important words from the story on the lines below.

1. Shep is a big dog. He stays outside. He chases cars. He barks at the squirrels. Ted plays with Shep.

2. Mitten is a black kitten. She has white feet. She stays in the house. She sleeps in a chair. She drinks milk. She purrs.

1. Shep

   is a big dog

   _____

   chases cars

   _____

   _____

2. Mitten

   _____

   has white feet

   _____

   _____

   drinks milk

   _____

Name _____

Read each part of the story. Write the answer to each question on the line that comes after it.

The Children's Pets

Tom has a baby duck. It is little and fluffy. It is yellow. The duck says quack.

What is Tom's pet?   I. _____

What size is it?   A. _____

What does it feel like?   B. _____

What color is it?   C. _____

What does it say?   D. _____

Pam has a tiny turtle. Its shell is hard. Its body is soft. It hides its head inside the shell.

What is Pam's pet?   II. _____

What size is it?   A. _____

What covers it?   B. _____

What is soft?   C. _____

Where does it hide its head? D. _____

Name
_____

Read the story. Then fill in the lines on the outline. On each line, tell something about that kind of home.

Indian Homes

The Pueblo Indians lived in homes called **pueblos.** These homes were made of sun-dried earth called **adobe.** The roof of one was the floor of another.

Navajo Indians lived in homes called **hogans.** Hogans were made of logs covered with earth. They had dome-shaped roofs.

Indian Homes

I. Pueblo homes

  A. _____

  B. _____

II. Navajo homes

  A. _____

  B. _____

pueblo

hogan

Critical Thinking, Level B © 1993 Steck-Vaughn

Name _____

A. Classifying

Help! The circus wagon broke down! All the animals ran into the pet shop. Circle the animals that belong to the circus. Draw an **X** on the pet shop animals.

B. Definition and Example
Outlining and Summarizing

Finish the outline by writing the names of the animals that go with each definition. Use the **Word Box**.

I.   Wild animals used in circuses

    A. _____

    B. _____

II. Tame animals used as pets

    A. _____

    B. _____

Word Box

giraffe

puppy

elephant

kitten

Name _____

C. Fact and Opinion
Real and Make-Believe

Read the poems. Write **fact**, **opinion**, or **make-believe**.

A little egg
in a nest of hay.
Cheep-cheep.
Crack-crack.
A little chick
pecked his shell away.
Cheep-cheep.
Crack-crack.

A little white mouse
Playing on a sunbeam
Then sliding back down.

I am a nice boy
More than just nice,
Two million times more
The word is ADORABLE.

Look at the picture. What do you see? What can you imagine? Put your ideas into a poem. Write it on a sheet of paper.

Critical Thinking, Level B © 1993 Steck-Vaughn

Name

Understanding

Understanding means telling about something in your own words. Look at the picture. What are the man and the boy doing? What do you think they are talking about? Do you think they know each other? Why or why not?

For each row, write the letter of the one that is different.

1.
   A   B   C   D   _____

2.
   A   B   C   D   _____

3.
   A   B   C   D   _____

4.
   A   B   C   D   _____

5.
   A   B   C   D   _____

6.
   A   B   C   D   _____

Name _____

Read each question. Put a line under the best answer.

1. How are teachers, farmers, and doctors alike?
   They all work outdoors.   They are all people.
   They all go to school.

2. How are cabins, houses, and tents alike?
   They can be moved.   They all have fireplaces.
   You can live in them.

3. How are palm trees, apple trees, and grass alike?
   They are very tall.   They stay green all winter.
   They are plants.

4. How are kittens, calves, and puppies alike?
   They are young animals.   They are house pets.
   They are the same size.

5. How are trucks, tractors, and cars alike?
   They all stay outdoors.   They all have wheels.
   They are used only on farms.

6. How are chalk, pencils, and pens alike?
   They are used for writing.   They are all sharp.
   They all have erasers on them.

7. How are scissors, needles, and thread alike?
   They all cut.   They are used for sewing.
   They are all used for cooking.

Name

On each blank line, write a word from the **Word Box**.

Word Box

birds	beak	little	two	short

Both of these animals are _____ . One bird is

big. The other bird is _____ . One bird has long

feathers. The other bird has _____ feathers.

Each bird has _____ feet and a _____ .

Name _____

A. Houses have special parts outside. Look at the parts listed below. Write the number of each part to show where it belongs on the house.

1. door   4. window

2. roof   5. steps

3. brick   6. chimney

B. Houses also have special parts inside. Here is the inside of a house. Write the number of each part on the picture to show where it belongs.

1. ceiling   4. curtains

2. floor   5. fireplace

3. wall   6. bookcase

C. Write a word from the Word Box in each blank.

Word Box

carpet	paint	tile	wallpaper

Cover the inside walls of a house with _____ or

_____ . Cover the floors with _____ or

_____ .

Name _____

A. Different words may use the same letters. The order of the letters is different in these words: **tea, ate**. For each Pet Shop Word below, make another word. Use all the letters. The first one is done for you.

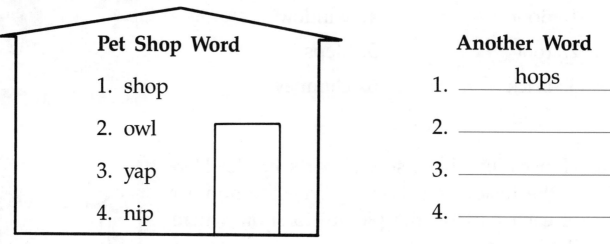

Pet Shop Word	Another Word
1. shop	1. hops
2. owl	2. _____
3. yap	3. _____
4. nip	4. _____

B. With some words, you can change one letter to make a new word. Change just one letter in each word on the Dog Word list to make another word that goes with the definition. The first one is done for you.

Dog Word	Definition	New Word
1. puppy	a kind of flower	1. poppy
2. fur	belonging to us	2. _____
3. bark	a farm building	3. _____
4. ball	something to ring	4. _____

Name _____

Read the story. Number the pictures in order.

On Saturday morning, Jimmy got up, brushed his teeth, and got dressed. Mother said that breakfast was ready. Jimmy ate breakfast. Then he played outdoors with his sister Alice. When Leon came along, all three children played together.

_____

_____

_____

_____

Name

Read the story. Then number the pictures in order. Use the numbers **1, 2, 3, 4,** and **5.**

Inez decided to make a sock puppet. She used an old sock that she found in her drawer. She cut dog ears out of a piece of brown felt. She glued one ear on each side of the sock. With red and brown markers she drew a dog mouth and nose on the sock. Then she glued on two blue buttons for eyes. When the glue was dry, Inez put her hand in the sock and used her puppet to tell a story.

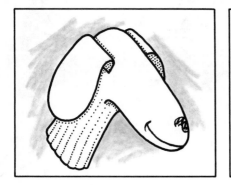 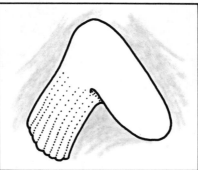 

_____   _____   _____

   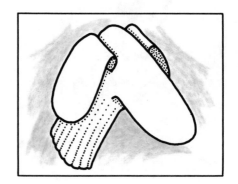

_____   _____

Name _____

Steps in a Process

Write **1**, **2**, and **3** to tell each story in order.

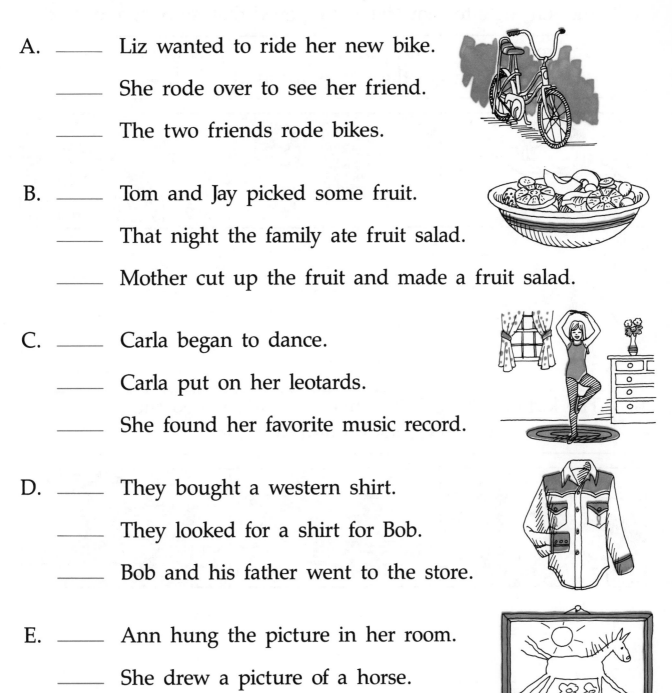

A. ⎯⎯ Liz wanted to ride her new bike.

⎯⎯ She rode over to see her friend.

⎯⎯ The two friends rode bikes.

B. ⎯⎯ Tom and Jay picked some fruit.

⎯⎯ That night the family ate fruit salad.

⎯⎯ Mother cut up the fruit and made a fruit salad.

C. ⎯⎯ Carla began to dance.

⎯⎯ Carla put on her leotards.

⎯⎯ She found her favorite music record.

D. ⎯⎯ They bought a western shirt.

⎯⎯ They looked for a shirt for Bob.

⎯⎯ Bob and his father went to the store.

E. ⎯⎯ Ann hung the picture in her room.

⎯⎯ She drew a picture of a horse.

⎯⎯ Ann took out her crayons and paper.

Name _____

Look at the story pictures and read the sentences in the box. Then write the sentences to show what happened first, second, and third.

A. | Tina made a sign and put it up.   Tina built the fort.
Tina got the things to build a fort.

1. _____

2. _____

3. _____

B. | The kitten got stuck in a tree.   He rescued the kitten.
Uncle Carlos brought a ladder.

1. _____

2. _____

3. _____

Name _____

Color this shape ☐ green.　　Color this shape ◯ orange.

Color this shape △ brown.　　Color this ▯ and this ☐ yellow.

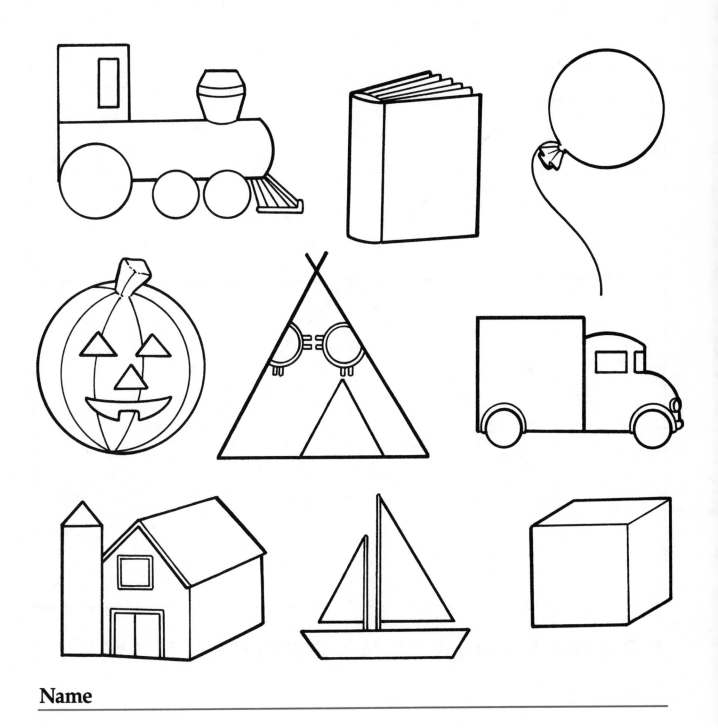

Name _____

Fourteen letters of the alphabet are hiding here!

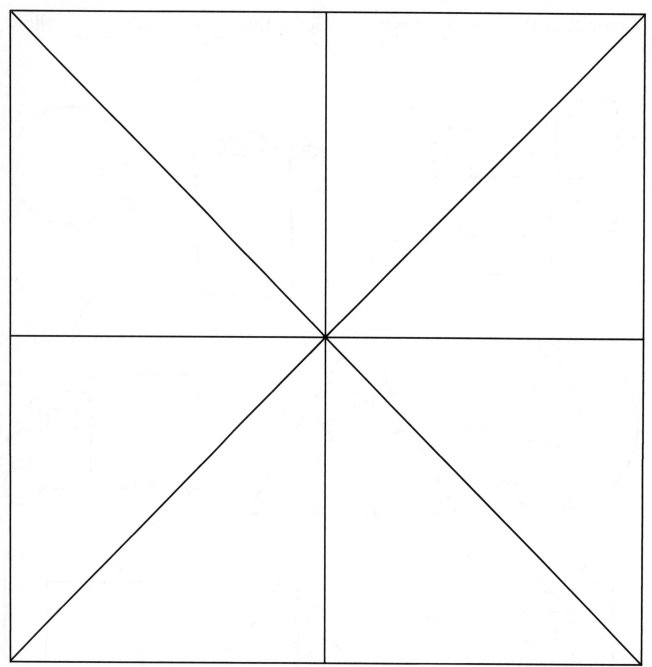

A B C D E F G H I J K L M N O P Q R S T U V W X Y Z

Name _____

Critical Thinking, Level B © 1993 Steck-Vaughn

Comparing Word Meanings

Write the word that means the same. Then write the word that means the opposite.

		Same	**Opposite**

A.

bad	same	bold	nice	afraid	different

1. brave _____ _____

2. alike _____ _____

3. good _____ _____

B.

dull	mend	big	shining	small	smash

1. little _____ _____

2. bright _____ _____

3. break _____ _____

C.

well	fast	tall	slow	short	ill

1. high _____ _____

2. quick _____ _____

3. sick _____ _____

Name

_____

In each blank, write the correct word from the **Word Box**.

Word Box

be	rode	flour	would	two	wood
to	road	bee	sun	flower	son

Examples: He is the youngest ___son___ of the family.

The ___sun___ is bright today.

1. May we go _____ the store?

2. Twins are _____ children who often look alike.

3. Jane _____ the horse for a long time.

4. The car was on the _____.

5. A tulip is a kind of _____.

6. I use _____ when I bake.

7. Lee wants to _____ a teacher.

8. The _____ stung me on the arm.

9. We _____ like to go with you.

10. The chair is made of _____.

Critical Thinking, Level B © 1993 Steck-Vaughn

Name

_____

Circle the best title for each story.

A.　Spot is a little gray pony. He lives on a farm. One day, Mei was riding Spot. Spot stepped into a hole. He hurt his leg. The doctor had to fix it.

1. Spot's Hurt Leg
2. Mei Loves Spot
3. A Little Gray Pony

B.　The turtle and the hippo had a race. The hippo went faster than the turtle. It finished the race before the turtle did. The turtle said, "I enjoyed our race."

1. Angry Turtle
2. The Speedy Hippo
3. The Elephant's Friends

C.　People keep many kinds of pets in their homes. Some have dogs or cats. Others have birds or fish. Some people even have tame monkeys!

1. Sally's Pets
2. People Need Pets
3. Kinds of House Pets

Name

Read each story. Then underline the sentence in the box that tells the main idea.

1.   A cactus is a spiny plant. It grows in the desert. It needs very little water.

It is hot in the desert.
Cactus is a desert plant.

2.   Oranges grow on trees. First they are green. Then they turn yellow. At last they turn orange.

Oranges change color.
Oranges are juicy.

3.   The part of a carrot that you eat is the root. It grows under the ground. It has lacy green leaves on top.

Carrots taste good.
Carrots are root vegetables.

4.   Cotton grows in places where it is hot. It needs lots of sunshine and water. When the cotton pods get very big, they burst open.

Some clothes are made of cotton.
Cotton needs warm weather.

Name

Read each story. Circle the sentence that tells the main idea.

1. Jackie tied on her bonnet. Then she laced up her high-top shoes. Jackie was getting ready for a costume party.

2. The parade was so much fun! We saw floats and banners. There were clowns and bands. There were even dancing dogs.

3. First you see streaks of light. Then the sky gets lighter and lighter. A sunrise is very beautiful.

4. Mark wanted to paint a picture. He set up his easel and paints. He found paper and brushes. Then he spread paper on the floor.

Name

Circle the word that tells what the story is about. Then draw a line under the main idea sentence.

Example: (Kites) are lots of fun. You have to run fast to get them flying. Then the kites dance in the air.

1.   Here is how to make a mask. Get a big paper bag. Then use scissors to cut eyeholes. Use paint and yarn to finish the funny face.

2.   Skyrockets are beautiful. Their colors flash in the night sky. People enjoy watching the colors pop and drop through the dark.

3.   Tadpoles are young frogs. At first they look more like fish than frogs. They wiggle through the water. Soon they grow legs and can hop on the ground.

4.   Ben got a surprise for his birthday. The surprise was gray and white. The surprise said, "Meow." Ben gave the surprise a bowl of milk.

5.   Nancy filled the washtub with water. Next she found Bowser's soap and tub toy. Nancy was going to give her dog a bath.

6.   The sun gives us light. It makes the air warm. It helps things grow. The sun is important to everything on Earth.

Critical Thinking, Level B © 1993 Steck-Vaughn

Name

Identifying Relationships

Write a number to show where each person is going.

Name

Read each job name in the middle. Draw lines to show two things used by a person who does that job.

•   •   **police officer**   •   •

•   •   **firefighter**   •   •

•   •   **chef**   •   •

•   •   **carpenter**   •   •

•   •   **astronaut**   •   •

•   •   **nurse**   •   •

Name _____

Write the letter of the picture that will fill each blank correctly.

A   B   C   D

E   F   G   H

1. It is raining, so you will need an _____ if you go out.

2. If you want to color, you will need _____.

3. If you drop the _____, it will break.

4. Some people like to read, so they need _____.

5. If the _____ shines, the _____ will melt.

6. To catch a _____, you need a _____.

Name

Read each sentence. Fill in each blank with the correct word from the **Word Box**.

Word Box

| Tuesday | bat | pencil | nail | hungry | water |
| baseball | won | apple | out | party | red |

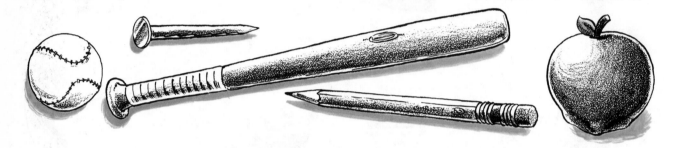

1. Eva ran faster than Sam, so Eva _____ the race.

2. Ben stepped on a rusty _____, so he went to the doctor.

3. Since the sun is _____, we can go on a picnic.

4. Tina wanted to write, so she got a _____.

5. It was John's birthday, so we gave him a _____.

6. Yesterday was Monday, so today must be _____.

7. Lucy lost her green socks, so she wore her _____ ones.

8. If you are thirsty, drink some _____.

9. To play _____, you need a _____.

10. Paul was _____, so he ate an _____.

Name _____

Critical Thinking, Level B © 1993 Steck-Vaughn

A. Identifying Relationships
Understanding Pictures

Draw a line from each sentence to the thing the animal needs.

The deer is thirsty.

The bird wants to build a nest.

The bee wants to fly home.

B. Steps in a Process
Identifying Main Ideas

The directions for building a doghouse are below, but they are all mixed up. Write **1** before the step that comes first, **2** before the second step, and so on.

_____ Build the roof.

_____ Get wood, hammers, and nails.

_____ Paint the doghouse.

_____ Build the sides of the house.

On the line below, write a title for your directions.

_____

Name _____

C. Identifying Structure

An animal name is hiding in each of the words below. Circle the letters that name the animal. The first one is done for you.

1. b(o x)   3. c a p e   5. s p i g o t

2. c r a t e   4. h e e l   6. l a n t e r n

D. Comparing and Contrasting
   Comparing Word Meanings

You can write some words so that they **look** like what they mean.

In the space below, write the following word pairs so they look like what they mean.

beautiful ugly   happy sad   straight bent

Name

Critical Thinking, Level B © 1993 Steck-Vaughn

Applying

Applying means using what you know. Let's try it out. Look at the picture. Did someone in the picture say something funny? How do you know? Do you think one of the girls told the joke? Why or why not?

Ordering Objects

Put the pictures in each row in order. The first picture has **1** under it. Write **2**, **3**, and **4** on the correct lines.

A.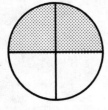

_____   _____   _____   **1**

B.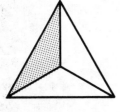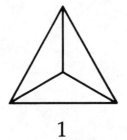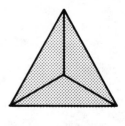

_____   _____   **1**   _____

C.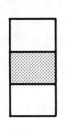

_____   **1**   _____   _____

D.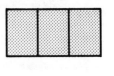

_____   _____   **1**   _____

Name _____

For each row decide what comes next. Draw it.

1.

2.

3.

4.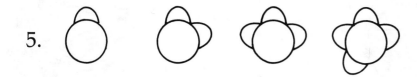

L M N O P Q R

5.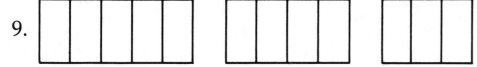

6. PxA PxB PxC PxD

7. 19 17 15 13 11 9

8.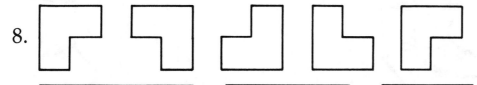

9.

Name

For each row, draw step 3.

A.

  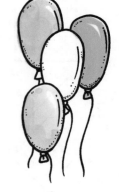

1.　　　　2.　　　　3.　　　　4.

B.

1.　　　　2.　　　　3.　　　　4.

C.

1.　　　　2.　　　　3.　　　　4.

Name

Will the things pictured on the right fit into the container?
If so, mark **X** on the line.

 _____

 _____

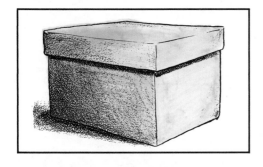 _____

 _____

Name _____

Circle the picture that answers each question.

1. Which ball will fit in the box?

2. Which mitten will fit best?

3. Which drapes will fit best on the window?

4. Which tie will fit best on the shirt?

5. Which saucer will fit best with the cup?

6. Which collar will fit best on the dog?

7. Which box will fit on the shelf?

Name

Study the map. Then answer the questions.

1. Whose house is closest to the store?

_____

2. Whose house is farthest from the school?

_____

3. Which is closer to the school—the pond or the park?

_____

4. Whose house is farthest from the restaurant?

_____

5. Who lives across the street from the post office and the library?

_____

Name _____

Circle the answer in each box that tells how long it would probably take to do each thing.

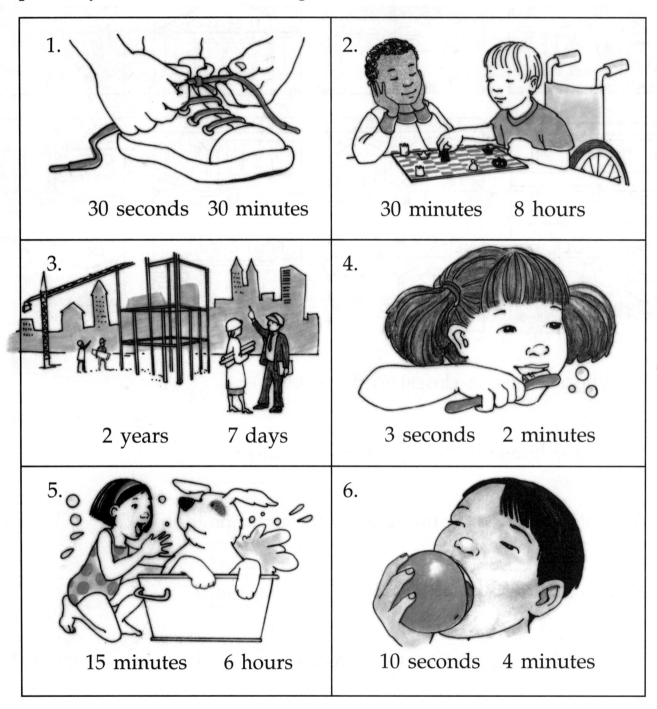

1. 30 seconds   30 minutes

2. 30 minutes   8 hours

3. 2 years   7 days

4. 3 seconds   2 minutes

5. 15 minutes   6 hours

6. 10 seconds   4 minutes

Critical Thinking, Level B © 1993 Steck-Vaughn

Name _____

Look at each set of pictures. Then read the three sentences.
Put an **X** before the sentence that tells what will happen next.

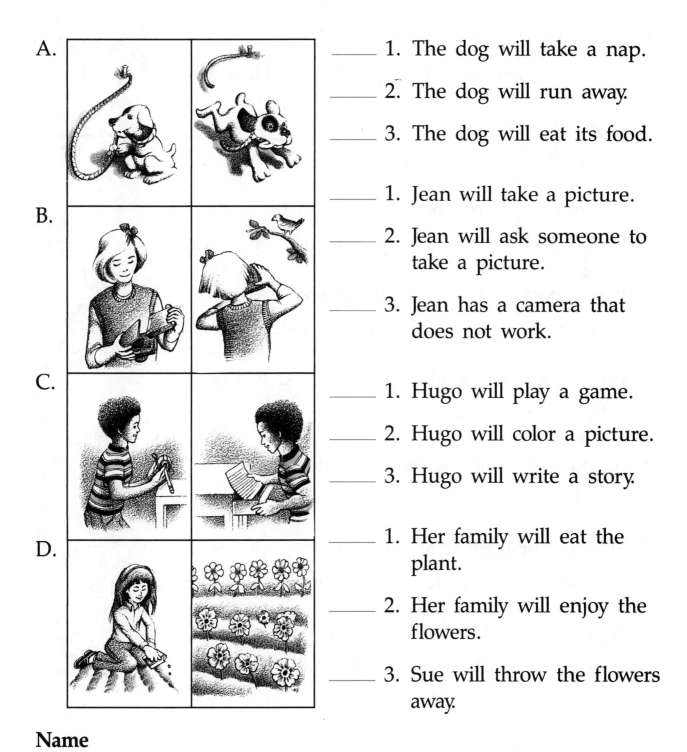

A.

_____ 1. The dog will take a nap.

_____ 2. The dog will run away.

_____ 3. The dog will eat its food.

B.

_____ 1. Jean will take a picture.

_____ 2. Jean will ask someone to take a picture.

_____ 3. Jean has a camera that does not work.

C.

_____ 1. Hugo will play a game.

_____ 2. Hugo will color a picture.

_____ 3. Hugo will write a story.

D.

_____ 1. Her family will eat the plant.

_____ 2. Her family will enjoy the flowers.

_____ 3. Sue will throw the flowers away.

Name

Read the beginning of each sentence. Circle the correct sentence ending.

1. If you plant a seed, it should

    die.   get smaller.   grow.   blow away.

2. When you write a word, you want others to

    read it.   cross it out.   erase it.   lose it.

3. When you go to a party, you want to

    be sad.   get sick.   go home.   have fun.

4. If you pack a suitcase, you are ready to

    go on a trip.   go to school.   eat.   get lost.

5. Pretend the temperature is zero. You will be

    hot.   warm.   cold.   cool.

6. If you lose some money, you will be

    sad.   glad.   happy.   tired.

7. When your team wins, you feel

    good.   bad.   silly.   sorry.

8. If you get a letter from a friend, you will

    lose it.   drop it.   find it.   read it.

Critical Thinking, Level B © 1993 Steck-Vaughn

Name

(Thinking About What Will Happen)

Read each sentence beginning. Finish the sentence in your own way.

1. If rabbits moved into my house, I would _____

_____ .

2. If a dog ate my boots, I would _____

_____ .

3. If a space creature came to my house, I would _____

_____ .

4. If I could ride in the space shuttle, I would _____

_____ .

5. If it snowed on the Fourth of July, I would _____

_____ .

Name _____

(Thinking About What Will Happen)

Put on your thinking cap! Ready? OK. Write sentences to answer these questions.

1. Do you think life on the earth would change if it stayed light 24 hours a day? How?

_____

_____

_____

2. If it never rained again, would it change the way we live? How?

_____

_____

_____

3. How would our lives change if we no longer had cars or buses or trains or planes?

_____

_____

_____

Name _____

Critical Thinking, Level B © 1993 Steck-Vaughn

Write **yes** if you are sure that the sentence is true. Write **no** if you cannot be sure that the sentence is true.

1.

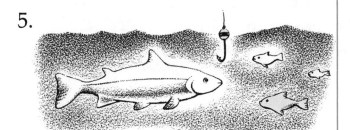

This ring could
belong only to Jane. _____

2.

Mary lives in this
apartment house. _____

3.

It is winter. _____

4.

The black horse
will win. _____

5.

Meili caught
this fish. _____

6.

The boy is riding
the bicycle. _____

Name _____

Read each story. Circle the picture that answers the question at the end of the story. Then put an **X** before the sentence that tells why you chose that picture.

A.   John was watching a TV show. A man was crossing the desert. John could almost feel the hot sun. Soon, John ran to get something he wanted very much. What do you think it was?

What makes you think so?

1. _____ When you cross a desert, you need something to ride on.

2. _____ John was thirsty. He felt as if he were trying to cross the desert, too.

3. _____ John was tired of watching TV and wanted to play.

B.   Mother needed to go shopping. She had a list and her purse. Mother got into the car. She could not start it. She asked Lupe to get something for her. What did Mother want Lupe to get?

What makes you think so?

1. _____ Mother wanted to buy toys.

2. _____ The box can carry the groceries.

3. _____ You need a key to start a car.

Name

Critical Thinking, Level B © 1993 Steck-Vaughn

Read each story. Then follow the directions.

A.   A woman left some letters at Dot's house. One was from Dot's uncle. Circle the name of the person who left the letters.

Dot's uncle
the mail carrier
Dot

Put an **X** in front of the reason for your choice.

1. _____ Dot lives there.

2. _____ Dot's uncle wrote the letter.

3. _____ The mail carrier delivers mail to houses.

B.   Jack said, "What am I thinking of? The animal has little front legs, long back legs, and a pocket. It hops around on its back legs." Circle the name of the animal Jack is thinking of.

a rabbit
a monkey
a kangaroo

Put an **X** in front of the reason for your choice.

1. _____ Monkeys have four long legs for swinging.

2. _____ Rabbits have strong back legs and long ears.

3. _____ Kangaroos have strong back legs and a pocket.

Name _____

Read each story. In the blank, write the correct word from the story.

1. Carlos was walking down the street. He saw something fall from a girl's purse. He found a dime on the sidewalk.

    A _____ fell from the purse.

2. Father told Sue to finish her work after dinner. Sue finished dinner. Now she has to finish her _____.

3. Tomatoes must be picked as soon as they ripen. The tomatoes are ripe now. They must be _____.

4. On Wednesday the school lunchroom serves pizza. Today is Wednesday. The children will have _____ for lunch.

5. Frank must shovel snow before he plays. He has shoveled the snow. Now Frank can _____.

Name _____

Read each sentence. Think about how the word **run** is used. Find that meaning in the box. Write its number on the line after the sentence.

A.

The stream runs under the bridge. _____

B.

Our house is on her run. _____

C.

Windmills can run. _____

D.
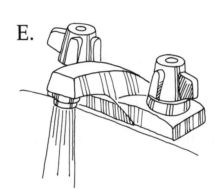
They can run an errand. _____

E.

The faucet runs. _____

F.
The boy runs. _____

Meanings

1. goes from one place to another
2. the water comes out
3. do something for someone
4. usual trip
5. go around
6. goes fast

Name _____

69

Read the words and their meanings. Then read each sentence. Put the letter of the correct meaning for each underlined word in front of each sentence.

Word Meanings

fly
A. insect with wings
B. move through the air with wings

roll
A. kind of bread
B. turn over and over

ring
A. give out a sound
B. thin circle of metal

_____ The fly landed on the flower.

_____ Birds fly south in the winter.

_____ Dad gave me a ring for my birthday.

_____ Did the phone ring?

_____ Maria wants a roll with her dinner.

_____ Let's roll down the hill.

Critical Thinking, Level B © 1993 Steck-Vaughn

Name _____

Read each sentence. Find a word in the **Word Box** that has the same meaning as the underlined words. Write the word on the line.

Word Box

| left | give | finished | help | come | watch | borrowed |

1. Mike took out a book. _____

2. Tina will lend a hand. _____

3. Hand over the jump rope to Jan. _____

4. Please keep an eye on the baby. _____

5. The airplane took off. _____

6. The game is all over. _____

7. Night has fallen. _____

Name _____

(Changes in Word Meanings)

Write a word from the box to finish each sentence. When you finish the story, go back and circle the correct meaning of each word.

bill	A. bird's beak	B. list of what is owed
pet	A. stroke or pat	B. animal kept by a person
left	A. opposite of <u>right</u>	B. went away from
pen	A. something for writing	B. fenced place for animals
line	A. long, thin mark	B. straight row

Miss Cody's class was excited. They were going to visit the children's zoo. They stood in a long _____ with other people at the gate. Once inside, they saw all kinds of animals. They went into a wooden _____ where there were friendly sheep. They admired the big bright _____ of a toucan in a huge bird cage. They even got to gently _____ a baby rabbit. They were very tired when they finally _____ the zoo at the day's end.

Name _____

A. Ordering Objects
Estimating
Inferring

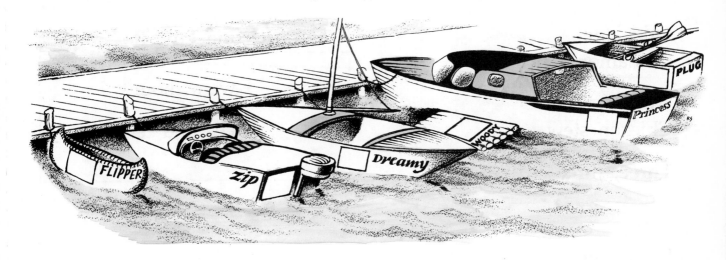

1. The boat race is about to start! First, the boats must line up according to size. Write **1** on the smallest boat, **2** on the next smallest, and so on up to **6**.

2. Look at **Zip** and **Princess**. Which one uses the most gas?

   _____

   Tell why you think so. _____

3. Look at **Flipper** and **Plug**. Which one can go faster if just one

   person is in it? _____

   Tell why you think so. _____

Name

B. Thinking About What Will Happen

Read the first two parts of the poem. Then finish the poem using the lines in the **Rhyme Line Box**.

One, **one**
Cinnamon **bun**

Two, **two**
Chicken **stew**

Three, three

_____

Four, four

_____

Rhyme Line Box

> I want more
>
> Cakes and tea

C. Changes in Word Meanings

It's fun to make up new words. Look at the new word one writer made up. Then make up your own new words to go in the sentences.

A **thrickle** is a tickle in the back of your throat.

1. The place where lost socks go is a _____.

2. The button on top of a baseball cap is a _____.

Name _____

Analyzing

Analyzing means seeing how parts fit together. What do you see in this picture? What is the girl doing? Why do you think she is drinking the water? Where is the water coming from? How do you know?

Judging Completeness

Finish drawing each picture.

Name

Read each sentence. Study the picture. Complete the sentence with a word from the **Word Box**.

Word Box

hands	wheel	door	picture	handle	short

1. The frame has no

   _____ .

2. The wagon needs a

   _____ .

3. One leg is too

   _____ .

4. The pitcher needs a

   _____ .

5. The house has no

   _____ .

6. The clock has no

   _____ .

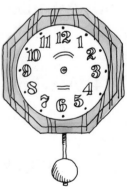

Name _____

(Judging Completeness)

A word is missing from each sentence below. Add a word from the box to complete each sentence and to tell about the picture. Write the new sentence.

| magician | acrobats | bicycle | rings | wire |

1. A little clown rode a huge.

_____

2. Three strong made a pyramid.

_____

3. A pulled an umbrella from a top hat.

_____

4. A woman walked on a up in the air.

_____

5. A juggler threw high into the air.

_____

Name

_____

Critical Thinking, Level B © 1993 Steck-Vaughn

For each part, put an **X** before the two things you feel are most important.

1. You are going to a friend's birthday party. You need to know

    _____ where the party will be.

    _____ what time the party will be.

    _____ how many people will be there.

2. You are going to the circus. You need to know

    _____ how to get there.

    _____ why a circus has animals.

    _____ how much it will cost.

3. You want to make a garden. You should know

    _____ how many of your friends eat vegetables.

    _____ how to plant a seed.

    _____ how often to water the garden.

4. Your friend will make a valentine. He will need

    _____ paste and scissors.

    _____ some kind of paper.

    _____ a book telling about holidays.

Name

A. Read the story.

Carol was going on a trip with her family. Who would take care of her little brown hamster while she was gone?

"I'll be glad to do that for you," said Carol's friend Lee.

Carol took her hamster to Lee's house. "This hamster's name is Wheelo," said Carol. "That's because his favorite toy is this wheel he runs around on. The main thing is to keep Wheelo healthy. He needs food three times a day. He needs water all the time. He has to be in a warm place."

"What's this little cage for?" asked Lee.

"You have to clean Wheelo's cage twice a week," said Carol. "Put him in the little cage while you clean his big one."

B. Put an **X** before the four most important rules.

Taking Care of a Hamster

1. _____ Feed it on time.

2. _____ Know the hamster's name.

3. _____ Keep the hamster warm.

4. _____ Give the hamster a wheel.

5. _____ Know the color of the hamster.

6. _____ Make sure the hamster has water.

7. _____ Play with the hamster.

8. _____ Clean the cage.

Name

Lisa is going to have a birthday party. Let's wrap some presents for her. Which things in the list below could you wrap and give to Lisa? Put an **X** before each one.

_____ a ring   _____ a toy car   _____ a dream

_____ fog   _____ a good idea   _____ a doll

_____ a nice time   _____ a purse   _____ an umbrella

_____ a skirt   _____ a little better   _____ a puzzle

_____ a smile   _____ noise   _____ a hat

_____ a baseball   _____ a game   _____ a watch

_____ a sunny day   _____ a week   _____ a lot of help

Name _____

Abstract or Concrete

Study the **Word Box**. On the lines in part 1, write words that name things you can only **think** about. In part 2, write words that name things you can **touch.**

Word Box

scarf	flower
pretty	button
silly	happy
mean	fish
idea	funny
angry	crayon
ball	busy
egg	bicycle
pen	kitten
lazy	pencil

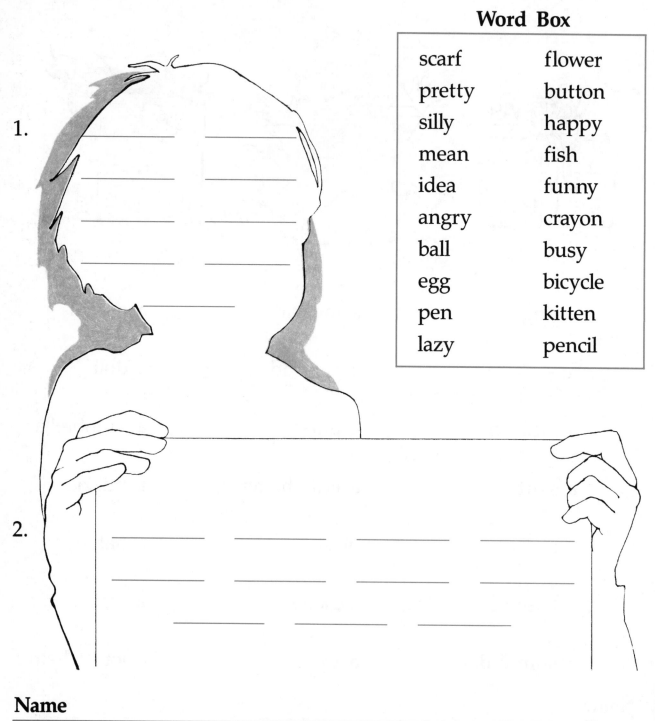

1.

2.

Name

Critical Thinking, Level B © © 1993 Steck-Vaughn

A. Look at the square at the right. Read about what it shows.

Joe's tennis shoe is part of a larger group of all tennis shoes. Tennis shoes are part of a larger group of all shoes. Shoes are part of a still larger group of all clothes.

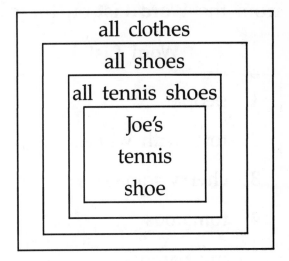

B. Write these words in the squares where they belong.

furniture   my rocking chair   oak trees

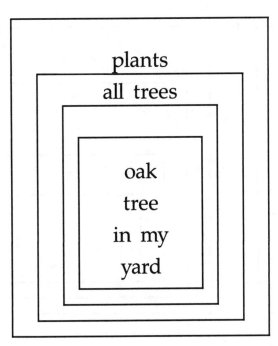

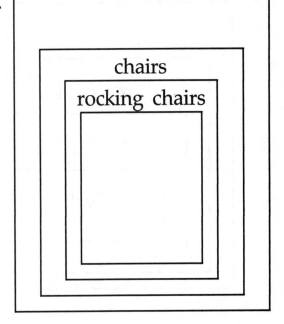

Name _____

Read the words in the squares and the **Word List**. Write words from the **Word List** on the correct lines inside the squares.

Word List

1. people
2. toys with wheels
3. cherry tomatoes
4. tomatoes
5. my parents
6. fruits and vegetables

A.
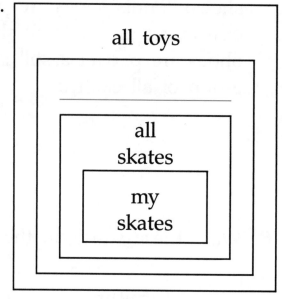

B.
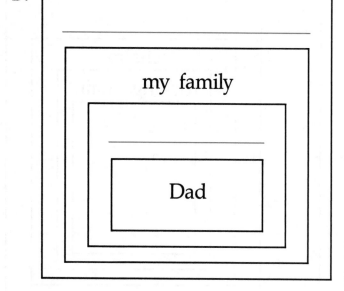

C.
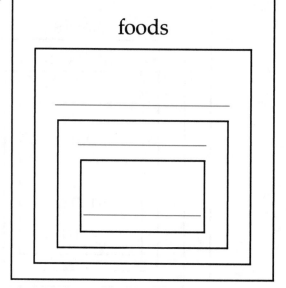

Critical Thinking, Level B © 1993 Steck-Vaughn

Name

84

A. Read each question. Find the answer in the Word Box. Write the word on the line.

kneel	run	jump	climb	sit

_____ 1. What do you do when you eat dinner?

_____ 2. What do you do if you want to go faster?

_____ 3. What must you do to paint the bottom of a door?

_____ 4. What do you do to go up?

_____ 5. What can you do with a rope?

B. Circle each thing someone might take on a camping trip.

Name _____

Look at the pictures and words under them. Read each sentence. If the boy could use **all three things** to do that job, draw a line under the sentence.

scissors   paint   glue

1. He could help fix a bulletin board.

2. He could fix breakfast.

3. He could decorate his toy box.

4. He could make a picture.

5. He could mow the grass.

6. He could make a get-well card.

7. He could make a storybook.

8. He could fix his wagon.

Name

Critical Thinking, Level B © 1993 Steck-Vaughn

A. Read the list of people's jobs in the box. Write the name of the person who would best solve each problem.

dentist	veterinarian	police officer
plumber	mechanic	doctor

1. You would call a _____ if you had a leaky sink.

2. You would call a _____ if you saw a lost child.

3. You would call a _____ if your dog was sick.

4. You would call a _____ if you weren't feeling well.

5. You would call a _____ if your car wouldn't start.

6. You would call a _____ if you had a tooth that hurt.

B. Finish each sentence by putting an **X** in front of the part that makes sense.

1. Mom's birthday is coming, so Peter should buy a _____ .

    _____ present for her   _____ book for himself

2. Maria's best friend is sick so she should _____ .

    _____ send a get well card   _____ invite her over this afternoon

3. Andres is leaving on a trip tomorrow so he should _____ .

    _____ go roller skating   _____ start packing a suitcase

Name

Find the word in each sentence that does **not** make sense. Circle it. Find a word in the **Word Box** that **would** make sense. Write it on the line.

_____ 1. Rita and Rudy ran to Mexico in a huge airplane.

_____ 2. Grandfather met them at the station.

_____ 3. Rita and Rudy visited a school while they were in Spain.

_____ 4. They made many new enemies in Mexico.

_____ 5. Rita and Rudy slept in a big school.

_____ 6. They got on the same train to go home.

_____ 7. They told friends at home about their circus.

_____ 8. The next year they rode a camel to Canada.

_____ 9. Rita and Rudy walked home in a car.

Word Box

friends
airplane
flew
hotel
trip
rode
airport
train
Mexico

Name _____

A. A story has characters.   WHO?
    A story has a setting.   WHERE?
    Read the story. Then follow your teacher's directions.

    The robot was standing in the toy store window. It didn't like it there. It wanted someone to take it home and play with it.

    Rosa walked by the store with her grandpa.

    "Oh, what a wonderful robot!" said Rosa.

    "I will get it for you for your birthday," said Grandpa.

    Grandpa and Rosa went into the store. Grandpa bought the robot. He and Rosa drove it home in the car. The robot enjoyed the ride.

    Rosa played with the robot. Now the robot was happy, and so was Rosa!

B. A story has action.   WHAT HAPPENED?
    Complete each sentence with a word from the story.

    1. Rosa wanted the _____.

    2. Rosa and Grandpa went into the _____.

    3. They took the new toy home in Grandpa's _____.

    4. Rosa played with the _____.

    5. Rosa felt _____.

Name _____

Read the story. Then follow your teacher's directions.

The school bus stopped at the corner. The bus driver looked around. Then the bus went on.

Brian saw the bus. Brian was running along the sidewalk. But he was not at the corner in time. Poor Brian! He missed the bus!

Brian stood on the corner. He had tears in his eyes. What should he do?

Then his mother came along in her car.

"What is wrong, Brian?" she asked.

"I missed the bus," Brian answered.

"Hop in. I'll take you to school." she said.

Critical Thinking, Level B © 1993 Steck-Vaughn

Name

A. Use the numbers 1-5 to show the story in order.
    Write the numbers on the lines under the pictures.

_____   _____   _____

_____   _____

B. What three things might the clown do after the show?
    Tell the things in order.

    1. _____

    2. _____

    3. _____

Name _____

91

Read the words in the **Word Box**. Then read the story. Write a word from the **Word Box** in each blank.

Word Box

path	noise	Jeff	glad
leaves	dark	walking	run
dog	feet	Rags	afraid

One day Jeff went _____ in the woods.

As he walked, he heard the dry _____ under his

_____. He saw many tall trees. It was _____

in the woods. Then _____ saw some big, round eyes.

They looked down at him. Jeff began to _____. He

was _____. A rabbit ran across his _____.

Then he heard another _____. It was his _____,

Rags. Jeff was _____ to see _____!

Name _____

If you said that something is either **here** or **gone**, you would be right. But, if you said that people have either brown or blue eyes, you would not be right. Some people have green eyes.

Put an **X** before each sentence that is not right because there may be more than two ways it can be.

_____ 1. A dog may be either black or white.

_____ 2. A branch may either have leaves or be bare.

_____ 3. A doctor may be either a man or a woman.

_____ 4. A safety pin may be either open or closed.

_____ 5. A baby may be either a boy or a girl.

_____ 6. Fruit may be either grapes or oranges.

_____ 7. You may go either up or down on a ladder.

_____ 8. Water may be either hot or cold.

Name _____

Put **X** before each sentence that is probably not all true. Then underline the word that could be changed to make the sentence true.

—— 1. Roy's parents let all the kids play in their yard.

—— 2. They can always go swimming.

—— 3. Some children have pets.

—— 4. Nine people are going on this trip.

—— 5. This is the best cereal of all.

—— 6. All of Mike's clothes are new, so why can't I have some?

—— 7. We're the only ones that don't have a swimming pool.

—— 8. There will be a big circus in town soon.

—— 9. Nobody will be wearing dresses to the party.

—— 10. Everybody knows that joke.

Name

A. Judging Completeness

Three people have forgotten to put on a part of their special suits. Draw the missing things where they belong.

B. Thinking About Facts That Fit

Imagine the captain asks you to come on the flight. Write a question you would ask before saying **yes** or **no**.

_____

C. Logic of Actions

Suzi will be a reporter on the space trip. When she returns, she will tell her classmates about the trip, and show them pictures. Name two things she should take.

_____   _____

Name _____

D. Story Logic
   Parts of a Story
   Recognizing True and False

Read the poem. Then answer the questions.

Pie Problem

If I eat one more piece of pie, I'll die!
If I can't have one more piece of pie, I'll die!
So since it's all decided I must die,
I might as well have one more piece of pie.
MMMM—OOH—MY!
Chomp—Gulp—'Bye.

Shel Silverstein from A LIGHT IN THE ATTIC

1. Has the speaker eaten any pie yet? _____

2. Could the speaker really die? _____

3. What happened at the end of the poem?

_____

E. Abstract or Concrete

Write your own poem on a sheet of paper. Tell about something you cannot hold or touch. Use the Idea Box to help you get started.

Idea Box

friendship
love   fear
anger

Name _____

Critical Thinking, Level B © 1993 Steck-Vaughn